Jonah Peretti: Architect of the Internet Age

The Rise of a Media Innovator Who

Changed the Rules of Engagement

Sean Bevan

Disclaimer

The following book is for informational and educational purposes only. The information presented is without contract or any type of guarantee assurance. While every caution has been taken to provide accurate and current information, it is solely the reader's responsibility to check all information contained in this article before relying upon it. Neither the author nor the publisher can be held accountable for any errors or omissions. Under no circumstances will any legal responsibility or blame be held against the author or publisher for any reparation, damages, or monetary loss due to the information presented, either directly or indirectly. This book is not intended as legal or medical advice. If any such specialized advice is needed, seek a qualified individual for help.

Trademarks are used without permission. Use of the trademark is not authorized by, associated with, or sponsored by the trademark owners. All trademarks and brands used within this book are used with no intent to infringe on the trademark owners and are only used for clarifying purposes.

This book is an original work and is not affiliated with, sponsored by, or endorsed by any investors, media innovators, technology companies, production teams, or related individuals.

TABLE OF CONTENT

INTRODUCTION

In the evolving universe of digital media, where attention spans shrink and trends shift in a blink, few figures have exerted as profound an influence as Jonah Peretti. His story is not merely one of entrepreneurial success but of fundamentally altering how information, humor, and culture move across the internet. Born in Oakland, California, he would rise to become one of the most recognizable architects of the viral age, with ventures that permanently shifted the relationship between technology, content, and society.

Raised in a household deeply connected to the world of ideas, Jonah was exposed early to a combination of intellectual rigor and creativity. His mother, an Italian-American schoolteacher, and his father, a Jewish criminal defense lawyer, encouraged inquiry and debate. The blend of analytical thinking and expressive freedom would shape the course of his life and professional ambitions. Jonah's half-brother, comedian and writer

Chelsea Peretti, would also find her own path in shaping modern culture, though through a different medium.

In 1996, Jonah Peretti graduated from the University of California, Santa Cruz, with a degree in environmental studies. The major may seem distant from digital media at first glance, but his experience at UC Santa Cruz was critical in shaping his understanding of systems — ecological, societal, and informational. It was during these years that he cultivated an interest in how ideas propagate, an early curiosity that would later crystallize into his groundbreaking theories about viral content.

Seeking to deepen his understanding of media and society, he enrolled in the Media Lab at the Massachusetts Institute of Technology (MIT), where he earned a master's degree. While at MIT in the early 2000s, he participated in an experiment that would catapult him into unexpected fame: the Nike email exchange. In 2001, after attempting to customize a pair of Nike sneakers with the word "sweatshop," he received a refusal from the company. Instead of accepting the corporate shutdown quietly, Jonah forwarded the email correspondence to a few friends. Within days, the exchange had spread across the internet, landing him on major media outlets such as The Today Show and Nightline.

This event was pivotal. It revealed to Jonah the unpredictable yet powerful nature of online sharing. What began as a personal act of protest became a global conversation, purely through digital word-of-mouth. The experience seared into his mind the idea that emotional engagement and shareability, rather than traditional notions of marketing or editorial gatekeeping, could drive massive attention.

After graduating from MIT, Jonah's interests continued to mature, steering him toward the burgeoning intersections of technology and culture. In 2005, together with Kenneth Lerer and Andrew Breitbart, he co-founded 'The Huffington Post.' The website, launched on May 9, 2005, was initially positioned as a liberal counterweight to conservative aggregators like

'The Drudge Report.' His focus was less on political ideology and more on the mechanics of distribution — how articles could be engineered for maximum shareability across a range of emerging online platforms.

At The Huffington Post, Jonah perfected techniques for "content repackaging"—crafting" headlines, visuals, and summaries that traveled efficiently across the newly dominant social networks and email chains. Under his influence, the site expanded rapidly, reaching a peak where it attracted over 25 million unique visitors a month. Though Arianna Huffington was the face and public persona of the brand, Peretti was the architect behind much of its viral strategy, overseeing product development and user experience.

His success at The Huffington Post did not satisfy his hunger for experimentation. Jonah recognized that traditional media structures were being upended at an accelerating pace, and he believed that media companies needed to be built from the ground up with digital virality as their foundation. In November 2006, he left

The Huffington Post to incubate a new project that would fully embody his evolving vision: BuzzFeed.

BuzzFeed officially launched in 2006, but the early version bore little resemblance to the global media powerhouse it would later become. Initially operating as a "viral lab," BuzzFeed's mission was to track and predict the spread of content across the web. Jonah and his small team developed algorithms that identified which stories, memes, and videos were likely to break out based on early indicators of popularity. The site primarily served as a lab, not a destination, offering brands and publishers insights into digital trends.

By 2011, he had decided to pivot BuzzFeed into a full-fledged media company. Recognizing that the web's future would be dominated by "native" content"—articles, videos, and quizzes designed explicitly for social sharing — he directed BuzzFeed toward original content creation. He recruited high-profile journalists, including Ben Smith from 'Politico,' who became BuzzFeed's editor-in-chief in

December 2011. This move marked a significant moment: BuzzFeed was no longer just a meme aggregator but was serious about journalism.

The timing of BuzzFeed's transformation coincided with the explosion of social platforms like Facebook, Twitter, and later Instagram. Peretti instinctively understood the new landscape. Traditional news organizations were still treating social media as a promotional tool; BuzzFeed treated it as the primary distribution channel. Headlines were crafted to evoke emotional reactions — surprise, outrage, humor — and the articles themselves were structured for easy consumption and easy sharing.

One of Jonah's core insights was the realization that people do not share news articles solely because they are important; they share them because doing so says something about who they are. Sharing is an act of self-expression. With this in mind, BuzzFeed mastered the art of creating content that served users' desire to entertain, educate, or impress their social circles.

BuzzFeed's success was meteoric. By 2014, it was valued at nearly $1 billion after a $50 million investment from Andreessen Horowitz, a prominent venture capital firm. The site boasted over 200 million monthly unique visitors and had expanded into serious investigative journalism, listicles, and entertainment. It spawned hit franchises like BuzzFeed News, Tasty, and BuzzFeed Video. Its content reached billions globally, influencing politics, pop culture, and commerce.

Throughout this ascent, Jonah Peretti maintained a relatively low profile compared to other media CEOs. His focus remained squarely on systems, incentives, and data rather than personal brand building. His leadership style was analytical and experimental; he encouraged a culture where A/B testing and data-driven decision-making were the norms.

In 2016, BuzzFeed's reach and relevance were demonstrated vividly during the U.S. presidential election. BuzzFeed News produced major investigative pieces, and its viral political coverage played an undeniable role in shaping public discourse. Critics sometimes accused the site of blurring the lines between entertainment and journalism, but Jonah defended BuzzFeed's model as an honest reflection of how modern audiences consume information.

BuzzFeed continued to expand internationally, launching editions in the United Kingdom, Australia, Mexico, Japan, and Germany, among others. The company also experimented with new forms of media, including podcasts and television. In 2018, BuzzFeed News was awarded a National Magazine Award for its investigation into surveillance technology and global authoritarianism, marking a significant validation of his belief that viral platforms could also produce serious journalism.

Yet, the digital media landscape was changing rapidly. By the late 2010s, reliance on Facebook and other social networks for distribution became a liability. Algorithm changes, especially Facebook's 2018 pivot toward "meaningful social interactions," severely impacted traffic to many publishers, including BuzzFeed. The company faced layoffs in early 2019, cutting around 15% of its workforce, or roughly 200 employees. Jonah responded by calling for a coalition of digital media companies to negotiate better terms with tech giants, arguing that platforms should share revenue more fairly with content creators.

In December 2020, BuzzFeed acquired HuffPost from Verizon Media, bringing his career full circle. The move was part of a broader strategy to consolidate and stabilize digital media amid industry-wide challenges. In an internal memo, Jonah explained that combining the two companies would create a more sustainable business model, leveraging shared resources while preserving editorial independence.

BuzzFeed went public via a SPAC (special-purpose acquisition company) merger in December 2021, trading under the ticker symbol BZFD. The move was met with mixed reactions. While it validated BuzzFeed's status as a major media company, its stock performance faltered, reflecting broader investor skepticism about the profitability of digital journalism. He acknowledged the tough environment but remained committed to his vision of building a resilient, diversified media brand that could thrive in the changing landscape.

Even as BuzzFeed faced financial pressures, it remained culturally influential. New verticals like Complex Networks, which BuzzFeed acquired in 2021, expanded the company's reach into youth culture and commerce. Jonah's long-standing strategy of blending content with commerce — for instance, shoppable recipes in Tasty or branded quizzes — positioned BuzzFeed uniquely compared to traditional newsrooms.

Jonah Peretti's contributions to modern media cannot be overstated. He redefined what it meant to create and share content in an interconnected world. His insights into human psychology, platform dynamics, and digital systems built new pathways for information to travel, reshaping public discourse along the way.

Unlike many of his Silicon Valley contemporaries, he approached media with an artist's appreciation for culture and a scientist's obsession with systems. He was neither utopian nor cynical about the internet's possibilities; instead, he saw it as a dynamic organism, capable of spreading both trivial memes and critical truths. His work has illuminated how ideas move, mutate, and influence societies at scale.

At a time when trust in media is under strain and the future of journalism remains uncertain, Jonah Peretti's career offers both inspiration and caution. His early experiments with viral mechanics liberated creativity and gave rise to new voices. Yet, the same forces that enabled BuzzFeed's rise also contributed to the spread of misinformation and the fragmentation of public discourse.

The world Jonah Peretti helped create is complicated, exhilarating, and fraught with contradictions. His impact, however, is undeniable. As digital landscapes continue to evolve, the fingerprints of his ideas will remain imprinted on every viral tweet, every shared video, and every headline designed not just to inform but to connect, entertain, and provoke.

He is, and remains, one of the true visionaries of the internet age — a viral visionary whose influence has shaped not only what people consume but also how they understand and participate in the modern world.

CHAPTER 1: FROM OAKLAND ROOTS TO MIT DREAMS

The seeds of Jonah Peretti's future influence on global media were planted far from the bright lights of Manhattan boardrooms or Silicon Valley campuses. They were sown in Oakland, California, a city whose complexity, vibrancy, and contradictions would deeply shape his worldview. Born on January 1, 1974, Jonah grew up amid the social, racial, and economic dynamics that characterized Oakland in the 1970s and 1980s, a city brimming with creativity but also wrestling with systemic challenges.

His parents were a powerful intellectual force in his life. His father, a Jewish criminal defense lawyer, practiced law with a fierce commitment to civil liberties and social justice. His mother, an Italian-American schoolteacher, nurtured curiosity and critical thinking in her children.

The blend of advocacy, teaching, and intellectual freedom shaped Jonah's earliest understanding of the world. In a home where ideas were debated at the dinner table and social issues were part of everyday conversation, young Jonah learned early that information had power — not just to inform, but to move people.

Family life also included a strong dose of creativity. His younger half-sister, Chelsea Peretti, would later become a famous comedian, writer, and actress, best known for her role on the sitcom Brooklyn Nine-Nine. The Peretti household encouraged individualism and expression, planting the notion that personal voice could influence broader culture — a belief Jonah would carry with him into his professional life.

Growing up in Oakland exposed Jonah to a wide range of cultural influences. The city was an epicenter for progressive movements and multicultural exchange, a backdrop that left an indelible imprint. It was a place where ideas were contested openly and where creativity and activism often intertwined. From an early age, Jonah observed how messages could galvanize communities and how slogans, stories, and images could travel from protest marches to public consciousness almost by osmosis.

During his high school years, he attended the College Preparatory School, a private school in Oakland known for its rigorous academic standards and emphasis on critical thinking. His experiences there cemented a lifelong love of analysis, synthesis, and debate. Friends and teachers noticed early on that he had an unusual ability to see patterns — not only in data but also in human behavior. Whether discussing literature, politics, or technology, he approached subjects with a mix of creativity and methodical thinking that set him apart.

Upon graduating from high school in the early 1990s, Jonah chose to attend the University of California, Santa Cruz. The school's reputation for countercultural spirit and academic freedom suited him perfectly. At UC Santa Cruz, he majored in environmental studies, a discipline that might seem unrelated to digital media at first glance.

However, the connections were profound. Environmental studies forced Jonah to think about ecosystems — complex, interconnected systems in which small changes could produce cascading effects. This systems-based thinking would later underpin his understanding of the internet as a living, breathing network of human interaction.

At UC Santa Cruz, he also began to develop a fascination with technology's role in shaping communication. Email was just becoming widespread among students and academics, and the early architecture of the internet was still an open frontier. He saw possibilities where others saw novelty. He became intrigued not just by what people were saying online, but by how ideas, jokes, rumors, and movements could propagate almost organically through digital networks.

After graduating from UC Santa Cruz in 1996, Jonah faced a crossroads. Though he had a strong academic foundation and a growing curiosity about digital culture, he lacked technical training. He decided to bridge that gap by enrolling at the Massachusetts Institute of Technology (MIT), one of the most prestigious technology institutions in the world. Accepted into the Media Lab — an interdisciplinary research center focused on the convergence of technology, multimedia, and design — he entered a rarefied intellectual environment that would profoundly influence his career.

MIT's Media Lab, founded in 1985 by Nicholas Negroponte, was a place where traditional disciplinary boundaries broke down. Engineers, artists, computer scientists, and sociologists collaborated freely. Projects ranged from wearable computing to digital storytelling to artificial intelligence. The Media Lab was not concerned with publishing academic papers so much as building prototypes that pushed the edges of what technology could do.

At the Media Lab, Jonah was surrounded by innovators who were not merely theorizing about the future — they were building it. The atmosphere was electric, filled with a sense that traditional rules could be rewritten. It was here that Jonah sharpened his technical skills, learning about programming, networks, and interactive design. But it was also here that he began to articulate his most important insights: that ideas could move through networks in ways that mimicked biological phenomena — spreading, mutating, reproducing, and sometimes, dominating ecosystems entirely.

One of his earliest and most formative experiments at MIT came through a simple act of consumer activism that unexpectedly revealed the dynamics of digital virality. In late 2000, while ordering customized Nike sneakers online, he attempted to embroider the word "sweatshop" on the shoes. Nike rejected his request, citing a violation of corporate policy. Rather than accept the decision silently, he forwarded the email exchange to a few friends.

What happened next was astonishing. Within days, the email chain had been forwarded thousands of times. News outlets picked up the story. Jonah was invited to appear on The Today Show in early 2001. The exchange was discussed in classrooms, offices, and online forums. In an era before Twitter and Facebook, the story's spread demonstrated the enormous, untapped power of digital peer-to-peer communication.

This incident crystallized many of the concepts Jonah had been studying abstractly at MIT. He saw firsthand that an emotional hook — humor, outrage, or surprise — combined with easy distribution mechanisms could lead to exponential sharing. Importantly, it was not a major media outlet that had propelled the story into public consciousness; it was ordinary people sharing because the message resonated with them personally.

He began thinking systematically about these phenomena. He theorized that digital environments were governed by new sets of "virality laws" that did not apply to traditional media. In the old world, gatekeepers like newspaper editors decided which stories reached the public. In the new world, the public themselves could elevate a message — provided it was crafted in a way that resonated deeply and was frictionless to share.

At the Media Lab, Jonah collaborated with other researchers who were investigating similar themes. The atmosphere encouraged interdisciplinary mashups, and Jonah found himself in conversations about computational social science, memetics, and behavioral economics. His coursework and independent research culminated in projects that blended software, psychology, and culture in ways that anticipated the future direction of digital media.

Another important development during his time at MIT was Jonah's growing interest in the idea of platforms. He understood that the architecture of a platform — its design, incentives, and user controls — could dramatically shape how content spread. This insight would later influence BuzzFeed's entire operational model, as the company engineered its articles and videos specifically for the sharing behaviors encouraged by platforms like Facebook and Twitter.

While still at MIT, Jonah also contributed to the founding of 'ReBlog,' an early effort to create automated tools for aggregating blog content. Although it never achieved mass adoption, ReBlog represented a significant step in Jonah's thinking about how content could be curated, organized, and amplified at scale.

By the time Jonah graduated from MIT in 2001, the dot-com bubble had burst. Many of his contemporaries were struggling to find jobs or were abandoning internet projects entirely. But he remained convinced that the internet's fundamental dynamics were sound — it was only the initial wave of business models that had been flawed. He saw a future where the internet would not only survive but would become the dominant channel for human communication and culture.

Armed with his experiences from Oakland, his systems-thinking training at UC Santa Cruz, and his technical and conceptual education at MIT, Jonah Peretti was uniquely prepared for what came next. He was not interested merely in using the internet to distribute existing media products. He wanted to create a new kind of media altogether — one that recognized how ideas could be engineered for maximum impact in a digital ecosystem where emotional resonance, frictionless sharing, and platform dynamics ruled.

The early 2000s were a time of tremendous possibility but also uncertainty. He chose not to pursue the typical academic route, despite encouragement from some of his mentors. Nor did he follow the traditional tech startup path of creating consumer software or hardware products. Instead, he embarked on a quest to apply his theories about viral content to real-world ventures, starting with *The Huffington Post* and later, BuzzFeed.

But even in these early years, the blueprint was already forming. Jonah Peretti had seen something most others had missed: that in the internet age, the true power lay not just in creating content, but in understanding and influencing the pathways through which content traveled.

The ideas he cultivated at MIT would serve as the backbone for an entire career spent not just adapting to the digital era but actively shaping it — one meme, one article, one viral moment at a time.

CHAPTER 2: THE SWEATSHOP EMAIL THAT SPARKED A REVOLUTION

In the year 2000, Jonah Peretti was a graduate student at the MIT Media Lab, deeply immersed in understanding the new architectures of digital communication. It was a time when the internet was still a sprawling frontier, lacking the streamlined platforms that would later dominate its landscape. Social media had not yet coalesced into the force it would soon become; instead, online culture thrived through email lists, bulletin boards, early blogging platforms, and grassroots virality.

Against this backdrop, an almost whimsical personal decision would permanently alter the trajectory of his life — and incidentally, reveal to the world the dormant, explosive power of digital word-of-mouth. It all started with a simple online order from Nike.

In late 2000, Nike offered customers the ability to customize their sneakers through a program called Nike iD. Shoppers could choose different colors and designs and, crucially, add personalized text to their shoes. It was a marketing innovation aimed at empowering consumers to feel more connected to the brand, but Nike had placed restrictions on offensive or inappropriate language to maintain control over their corporate image.

Jonah, curious about the system's boundaries, decided to put it to the test. Rather than writing a standard name or slogan on his shoes, he entered the word "sweatshop" into the custom text field — a pointed reference to the growing public criticism of Nike's labor practices at the time. Allegations had been mounting for years that the company was relying on sweatshop labor in developing countries, paying workers meager wages under harsh and unsafe conditions. Activists had held protests and launched boycotts, but Nike had continued to maintain a carefully polished public image.

Upon submitting his order, Jonah quickly received a response from Nike rejecting his customization request. Their email stated that the term "sweatshop" was inappropriate and violated their rules for customization. Rather than let the exchange end there, he decided to forward the email chain — including his original order and Nike's denial — to a handful of his friends. The action was casual, almost reflexive. It was not intended as a strategic act of activism nor a deliberate media stunt. It was, in his own words later, "just a funny thing" to share.

What followed was an eruption that even he could not have anticipated.

The forwarded email resonated deeply with people who received it. They found the exchange simultaneously humorous, subversive, and illuminating — a single piece of correspondence that punctured the slick surface of a global brand with sharp irony. The email was passed along from inbox to inbox, gathering momentum with every forward. Each recipient became an amplifier, distributing the story to their own circles.

Within a week, the Nike email was circulating far beyond Jonah's original circle of friends. It landed in thousands of inboxes across the country and even internationally. News outlets picked up the story. On January 17, 2001, 'The Wall Street Journal' reported on the incident, highlighting how a simple email exchange had exposed Nike's vulnerability in the digital age. He was invited to appear on NBC's 'The Today Show,' where he discussed the episode and its broader implications.

This moment revealed something profound about the new communications environment taking shape. Traditional media had historically operated under a "broadcast" model — a few centralized sources pushing content out to many passive consumers. What Jonah had stumbled into was something different: a decentralized, peer-to-peer distribution system where individuals, not institutions, decided what content was worth sharing.

The sweatshop email crystallized several key principles that would later underpin his approach to media:

- Emotional Resonance Drives Sharing. The email was not just informational; it carried emotional weight. It evoked humor, outrage, irony, and a sense of insider rebellion. People shared it not because it was newsworthy in a traditional sense, but because it made them feel something strong enough to pass it along.

- Frictionless Distribution is Critical. Email was ubiquitous and effortless to use. Forwarding a message required only a few clicks. The lack of friction in sharing allowed the message to propagate rapidly.

- Authenticity Beats Corporate Messaging. Nike's slick advertising could not compete with the raw authenticity of the email exchange. In an era where brands were carefully curated, the unfiltered nature of Jonah's correspondence felt more genuine — and therefore more powerful.

- Networks Are More Powerful Than Hierarchies. The spread of the email did not depend on approval from editors, producers, or corporate gatekeepers. It moved through informal social networks, driven entirely by the voluntary actions of individuals.

As Jonah reflected later, the episode taught him that ideas could "spread through the internet like a virus" if they tapped into the right emotional currents and social dynamics. The Nike email was, in effect, an early proof-of-concept for what would later be termed "virality," although at the time the vocabulary around such phenomena was still developing.

The incident also brought him his first taste of public controversy. Some commentators criticized him for what they saw as a stunt, arguing that he was undermining serious critiques of labor practices by reducing them to a joke. Others hailed him as a clever provocateur who had found a new way to hold corporations accountable. Jonah largely stayed above the fray, focusing instead on the underlying mechanisms that had made the email spread so widely.

Importantly, Jonah did not monetize the moment. He did not launch a merchandise line, start a consultancy, or attempt to profit off his sudden fame. Instead, he treated the experience as a learning opportunity, a real-world laboratory for understanding how ideas moved through the internet's social fabric.

At the same time, the Nike episode positioned him within a larger movement that was taking shape around "culture jamming"—the" act of subverting or parodying corporate advertising and mainstream cultural narratives. Groups like Adbusters, which had been active since the 1990s, sought to disrupt commercial messaging through satire, irony, and guerrilla communication tactics. His email was seen by some as an example of this ethos, although he was not formally affiliated with any such groups.

The exposure also connected Jonah with an emerging network of media innovators and entrepreneurs who recognized that the traditional media business was on the brink of massive change. Among those who took notice was Arianna Huffington, who would later partner with Jonah to co-found The Huffington Post in 2005.

In retrospect, the sweatshop email can be seen not just as an isolated incident but as the beginning of a career-long pattern. Jonah's genius would consistently lie in his ability to identify latent energies within the culture — emotions, jokes, anxieties, desires — and find ways to crystallize them into content that people felt compelled to share. He was less interested in broadcasting messages from a pedestal and more interested in building mechanisms that allowed messages to spread organically.

Another important dimension of the Nike email was the way it subtly shifted perceptions of corporate power. Prior to the digital era, large corporations like Nike had near-total control over their public image. They crafted carefully managed campaigns, employed armies of public relations professionals, and relied on traditional media partnerships to maintain brand integrity. The internet, he demonstrated, could bypass all of that. A single email from an ordinary individual could puncture a corporation's image more effectively than a multimillion-dollar ad campaign.

Nike, for its part, responded cautiously to the situation. They issued statements emphasizing their commitment to ethical labor practices, but the damage had already been done. The brand's reputation, particularly among younger, digitally savvy consumers, took a hit that could not be easily repaired.

The success of the sweatshop email also exposed a gap in traditional media's understanding of the internet. Many mainstream outlets covered the story in a perfunctory way, treating it as a quirky anecdote rather than grasping its larger significance. Jonah, however, understood instinctively that a shift was underway — a democratization of information flow that would upend industries far beyond sneaker manufacturing.

As the buzz around the sweatshop email eventually faded, he quietly returned to his research at MIT, armed with invaluable firsthand experience. He continued to think deeply about the structures that enabled viral transmission of content, refining his ideas about what would later become "contagious media." In 2002, he even co-founded a project called the Contagious Media Lab at Eyebeam, an art and technology center in New York City. There, he collaborated with other creatives to design experiments aimed at testing the principles of viral spread, treating content as a kind of scientific phenomenon to be studied, manipulated, and understood.

The Nike sweatshop email remains a pivotal event in Jonah Peretti's story not only because it brought him public recognition but because it revealed the enormous potential for a new kind of media logic — one that prioritized shareability, emotional engagement, and networked distribution over traditional models of broadcast control.

It also signaled to him that the future of influence would not belong to those who shouted the loudest, but to those who understood how to design content that people would want to whisper to one another — across emails, across platforms, across continents.

The revolution had begun with a single word stitched onto a sneaker: "sweatshop."

The rest would be history in the making.

CHAPTER 3: CO-FOUNDING THE HUFFINGTON POST

By 2003, Jonah Peretti's instincts about the future of digital communication had sharpened considerably. After his early experiments with contagious media at MIT and Eyebeam and the viral explosion of the Nike sweatshop email, he had come to a firm understanding: traditional media outlets were vulnerable. They were built for a different kind of world, one in which the flow of information was controlled from the top down. The internet had already started dismantling that model. What it lacked, however, was a centralized platform that could harness the new, chaotic dynamics of digital culture while still offering the credibility and structure associated with old-guard journalism.

In 2003, he was introduced to Arianna Huffington. At the time, Arianna was already a well-known political commentator and writer, having made a high-profile ideological shift from conservative circles to a more progressive stance. She recognized the limitations of the traditional opinion pages and saw an opportunity to create something more dynamic, inclusive, and immediate. Together with Andrew Breitbart, who was working as her researcher, and Kenneth Lerer, a media executive with deep experience, discussions began to solidify around a new kind of media company — one that would live entirely online.

The founding team was an unusual combination of personalities. Arianna brought star power and a vast network of political and media connections. Kenneth Lerer contributed business acumen and funding. Andrew Breitbart, despite his later fame as a right-wing media provocateur, was at the time focused on the mechanics of rapid content aggregation. Jonah Peretti, meanwhile, brought the most radical piece of the puzzle: a deep, instinctual understanding of virality and internet behavior.

The Huffington Post officially launched on May 9, 2005. At its core, the site was envisioned as a hybrid — part news aggregator, part blogging platform, and part original reporting outlet. It would combine curated links to existing news stories with original commentary from a wide variety of contributors, ranging from celebrities to academics to unknown but passionate bloggers.

In the beginning, the platform faced significant skepticism. Traditional journalists scoffed at the idea that a website so reliant on unpaid bloggers and aggregated content could seriously compete with established media outlets. Critics dismissed it as a "left-wing Drudge Report," a reference to the influential conservative news aggregator founded by Matt Drudge. Others derided it as nothing more than a vanity project for Arianna and her Hollywood friends.

The challenges were significant. First, there was the technical hurdle of building a platform that could scale. In the early days, the site struggled with server crashes when spikes in traffic occurred. Jonah, working largely behind the scenes, focused on engineering solutions that would allow the site to handle viral surges — a crucial lesson he had internalized from the Nike email experience. Scalability was not just a technical concern; it was a core strategic imperative.

Second, there was the question of credibility. The Huffington Post needed to establish itself not just as a clearinghouse for opinion but as a legitimate source of news and analysis. This required recruiting credible writers and editors, some of whom came from traditional media backgrounds. Over time, the site built up a roster of respected voices, blending them with celebrity bloggers like Larry David and Nora Ephron, whose posts attracted significant traffic and attention.

Jonah's influence on the editorial philosophy of the site was subtle but profound. He pushed for a model that understood content not merely as information but as a potential vector for social transmission. Headlines were crafted with an eye toward virality. Stories were framed to provoke emotional responses — outrage, humor, curiosity — that would compel sharing across email and, increasingly, on the nascent social media platforms like MySpace and early Facebook.

Another innovation was the comment section. Unlike traditional newspapers, which treated letters to the editor as an afterthought, The Huffington Post built its community features directly into the core of the site. Commenters could engage immediately with content, creating a feedback loop that increased time on site and deepened user investment. He recognized early on that the internet was not just a broadcast medium; it was a conversation.

Financially, the venture was modest at first. Arianna Huffington and Kenneth Lerer funded the initial launch out of pocket. But by the following year, The Huffington Post had raised its first outside investment: a $5 million Series A round led by SoftBank Capital in August 2006. The funding allowed for expansion, including hiring professional reporters and building out sections beyond politics, such as entertainment, lifestyle, and business.

The site's growth was rapid and undeniable. By 2007, The Huffington Post was one of the most trafficked political websites in the United States, surpassing many traditional outlets in online reach. Jonah, who by then held the title of Chief Technology Officer, continued to refine the platform's viral mechanics. He paid close attention to metrics, studying which stories caught fire and why. Data became as important to editorial strategy as traditional news judgment.

An important turning point came during the 2008 presidential election. The Huffington Post's coverage of Barack Obama's candidacy, and later his presidency, drove enormous traffic. The site positioned itself as a progressive counterweight to Fox News and other conservative outlets while still offering space for a diversity of voices. Jonah understood that major political events were opportunities for mass engagement — not just through formal news articles, but through blog posts, viral videos, photo galleries, and user-generated content.

One of the landmark moments during this period was the publication of a controversial blog post by actor and political activist George Clooney, although in that case the post had actually been compiled from his interviews rather than written directly by him, which led to some backlash. Nevertheless, it illustrated how The Huffington Post could leverage celebrity involvement to drive conversation — and clicks.

Another major milestone came in 2009, when The Huffington Post won its first significant journalism award: a Pulitzer Prize for David Wood's 10-part series on wounded veterans of Iraq and Afghanistan. It was a resounding validation that the site was not merely a platform for aggregated content or celebrity blogging; it was capable of producing serious, award-winning journalism.

Throughout this evolution, Jonah Peretti's focus remained on scale, engagement, and innovation. He was less interested in traditional prestige and more fascinated by the mechanics of how content could move through digital spaces. His background in contagious media gave him a unique perspective on what worked and what didn't. He encouraged experiments in headline testing, A/B experiments on story layouts, and new approaches to content packaging.

He also began to think beyond The Huffington Post. He realized that while The Huffington Post had successfully adapted old media values to a new media platform, there was room for an even more radical vision: a media company built entirely around the science of virality, without any lingering attachment to traditional journalism norms. In the background of The Huffington Post's success, the seeds for BuzzFeed were quietly germinating.

Still, The Huffington Post represented an enormous personal and professional triumph for Jonah. It proved that his theories about networked media were not merely academic; they could be operationalized into a successful, influential, and profitable enterprise. By 2011, The Huffington Post had achieved an online audience of over 25 million unique visitors per month, making it one of the top news destinations in the country.

That year, a major inflection point arrived: on February 7, 2011, AOL announced that it was purchasing The Huffington Post for $315 million. Arianna Huffington would stay on as president and editor-in-chief of The Huffington Post Media Group, which included AOL's other content properties like Engadget and TechCrunch. Jonah, however, chose not to follow. He had already begun transitioning his focus toward BuzzFeed, the company he had quietly founded in 2006 as a side project.

The AOL acquisition was a watershed moment for digital media. It demonstrated that online-native news organizations could achieve valuations once reserved only for legacy institutions. It also marked the beginning of a new era in which media companies were judged less by their prestige and more by their ability to generate engagement, audience growth, and virality.

For Jonah Peretti, co-founding The Huffington Post was more than just a business venture. It was full-scale proof that the dynamics he had studied, tested, and intuited — the emotional currents that drove people to share, the structures that allowed content to spread, and the architectures that favored conversation over lecture — could be the foundation for a new media empire.

He had helped create not just a website, but a blueprint for the future of journalism in the 21st century. And he was only just getting started.

CHAPTER 4: THE BIRTH OF BUZZFEED

By the mid-2000s, Jonah Peretti stood at a unique crossroads. The Huffington Post was rapidly establishing itself as a major online news destination, validated by soaring traffic numbers, awards, and a nine-figure acquisition on the horizon. Yet Jonah's mind, restless and wired for the future, was increasingly preoccupied with a different question: what if a media company were built entirely around the science of virality? Not merely adapting traditional media forms for the internet, but designing content from the ground up based on how people actually interacted with information online.

The origins of BuzzFeed trace back to 2006. At that time, he was still fully involved with The Huffington Post. But in the corners of his mind — and later, in the back room of a shared office space in New York's Chinatown — he began nurturing a side project. The initial idea was modest: a lab for studying and tracking viral trends across the internet. He envisioned a site that could map the spread of memes, news items, videos, and jokes as they flashed through emerging social networks.

He called it "BuzzFeed."

The name itself encapsulated the vision: "buzz" captured the viral energy of online culture, while "feed" suggested a constant, flowing stream of information. He secured an early partnership with John Johnson, co-founder of Eyebeam Art and Technology Center, where Jonah had previously worked after MIT. Johnson's company, Betaworks, provided seed funding and helped incubate the project. BuzzFeed was formally incorporated as a company in November 2006.

In its earliest days, BuzzFeed was less a media outlet than a research experiment. The initial team was tiny. Jonah Peretti, working alongside a handful of engineers, built simple tools to detect what was trending on the internet. They designed algorithms to scan forums, blogs, and early social media platforms for signs of virality. It was a passive operation at first — BuzzFeed wasn't creating content yet, only identifying it.

However, he quickly realized that merely tracking trends wasn't enough. The more powerful opportunity lay in creating the content that would become viral. Data could inform creativity. Science and art could be merged. This realization marked a critical pivot: BuzzFeed would not just observe the internet's viral forces. It would actively shape them.

In 2008, Jonah made a key hire that would accelerate this transformation: Peggy Wang, a former editor at the music blog Stereogum, became BuzzFeed's first editorial staffer. Her task was simple but revolutionary: use insights from BuzzFeed's data tools to create new pieces of content designed to resonate emotionally and socially.

The results were immediate. Lists, quizzes, and light-hearted posts proved extraordinarily shareable. Early successes like "21 Pictures That Will Restore Your Faith in Humanity" and "10 Puppies Who Forgot How To Dog" tapped into emotions — joy, nostalgia, awe —

that he knew were the engines of virality. BuzzFeed content was not optimized for SEO or clickbait in the traditional sense; it was optimized for sharing among friends.

Jonah's approach to scaling BuzzFeed was methodical. He formalized a content strategy around what he termed the "Bored-at-Work Network"—a" conceptual framework that recognized a massive, underutilized audience of office workers spending idle time on the internet during the workday. This audience wanted quick, engaging, emotionally resonant content they could consume and pass along easily. BuzzFeed's format — image-heavy, bite-sized, and mobile-friendly — was perfectly suited to meet this demand.

Meanwhile, social media platforms were undergoing their own transformations. Facebook had opened to the public in September 2006, and by 2009 it had become the primary driver of referral traffic for many websites. Twitter, launched in July 2006, was beginning to gain mainstream adoption. Jonah recognized early that the power balance was shifting: no longer would audiences find content by searching or browsing static homepages. Increasingly, content would find audiences through social feeds.

To capitalize on this shift, BuzzFeed doubled down on social distribution. Every article was crafted with sharing in mind. Headlines were punchy, visual elements were central, and calls to action subtly encouraged readers to post to their networks. Rather than chase Google rankings, BuzzFeed chased virality.

In 2010, BuzzFeed secured its first significant investment: a $3.5 million Series A round led by Hearst Ventures. The funding allowed Jonah to hire more writers, engineers, and designers, significantly expanding BuzzFeed's capabilities. Yet he remained cautious about growing too fast. He insisted that BuzzFeed focus on experimentation and learning rather than prematurely scaling a business model.

The next critical leap came with the decision to enter serious journalism. For all its success with lists, memes, and light-hearted content, he understood that BuzzFeed would not achieve long-term relevance unless it expanded its editorial scope. In January 2012, he hired Ben Smith, a respected political reporter from Politico, to be BuzzFeed's editor-in-chief.

The decision was transformative. Smith built a newsroom staffed with experienced journalists, many from traditional outlets. BuzzFeed began breaking real news, particularly in politics and culture. In the 2012 U.S. presidential election cycle, BuzzFeed's political team published scoops that were cited by major outlets and widely shared across social media. Jonah's vision was bearing out: a media company could be viral and serious at the same time.

By 2013, BuzzFeed's traffic was exploding. The site was reaching more than 100 million monthly unique visitors, and its content was regularly racking up millions of shares on Facebook and Twitter. Advertisers took notice. But BuzzFeed rejected the traditional display ad model — the clutter of banners and pop-ups that characterized much of web advertising at the time. Instead, Jonah pioneered the concept of "native advertising": sponsored content that was designed to blend seamlessly with editorial content, providing value to users rather than interrupting their experience.

This approach resonated with brands and audiences alike. BuzzFeed's advertising division grew rapidly, attracting major clients like GE, Virgin Mobile, and Taco Bell. In January 2013, BuzzFeed raised $19.3 million in a Series C round led by New Enterprise Associates, fueling further expansion into video, international markets, and new verticals like food, fashion, and tech.

One of Jonah's boldest moves was the creation of BuzzFeed Motion Pictures, launched in August 2014 under the leadership of Ze Frank. Located in Los Angeles, this division focused on producing original video content optimized for social media. It quickly became a powerhouse, generating billions of video views per month across Facebook, YouTube, Snapchat, and Instagram.

BuzzFeed's success culminated in a massive funding round in August 2015, when NBCUniversal invested $200 million, valuing the company at around $1.5 billion. A year later, NBCUniversal doubled down, investing another $200 million in October 2016, affirming BuzzFeed's status as a media giant.

Despite these achievements, Jonah never rested. He continually pushed BuzzFeed to innovate, expanding into areas like podcasting, investigative journalism, and even product development. He launched Tasty in July 2015, a food video brand that quickly became one of Facebook's most successful pages, spawning cookbooks, kitchen appliances, and licensing deals.

Under his leadership, BuzzFeed diversified aggressively. BuzzFeed News became a respected outlet, winning awards for investigations into topics like Russian propaganda and police misconduct. BuzzFeed Commerce experimented with product lines and affiliate marketing, reducing dependence on advertising.

BuzzFeed Studios pursued film and TV projects, extending the brand into traditional entertainment.

Yet challenges emerged as well. Changes to Facebook's algorithm in 2018 dramatically reduced organic reach for publishers, impacting BuzzFeed's traffic and revenue. Jonah responded by restructuring the company, laying off around 15% of staff in January 2019, while emphasizing direct-to-consumer businesses and new revenue streams.

Through it all, Jonah's guiding principles remained intact: understand how people behave online, create content that fits those behaviors, and build business models that align incentives between creators, audiences, and advertisers.

By the early 2020s, BuzzFeed stood as one of the few digital-native media companies that had survived the brutal shakeouts that claimed many of its peers. In June 2021, BuzzFeed announced plans to go public via a SPAC merger with 890 Fifth Avenue Partners, completing the deal in December 2021. It was a landmark moment: the first major pure-digital media company to make its debut on Wall Street.

Jonah Peretti's journey from MIT Media Lab tinkerer to CEO of a public company had taken nearly two decades. Along the way, he had reshaped not just how content was made and shared, but how media companies thought about their very purpose. BuzzFeed wasn't a fluke; it was the culmination of a long, thoughtful, experimental process — one driven by an unusually deep understanding of human psychology, technology, and culture.

The birth of BuzzFeed had proven that contagious media wasn't a side effect of the internet. It was its central organizing principle. And Jonah Peretti had built a company — and an empire — on that truth.

CHAPTER 5: MASTERING THE SCIENCE OF VIRALITY

Jonah Peretti did not stumble into the art of creating viral content. His success was not born from randomness or the whims of the internet, but from a disciplined study of patterns, behaviors, and emotional triggers that moved people to share. From the earliest stages of his career, Jonah believed that virality could be reverse-engineered — that human behavior on the internet followed recognizable, replicable patterns. He was not guessing. He was building a new kind of science.

By the time BuzzFeed was gaining traction in the late 2000s, Jonah had already spent more than a decade refining his thinking about why certain ideas spread while others fizzled. His early experiments at the MIT Media Lab in the late 1990s and early 2000s, particularly projects like the Reblogger tool he built at Eyebeam in 2002, had given him firsthand insight into the ways digital networks accelerated the sharing of information.

Yet it was at BuzzFeed where he had the freedom, resources, and scale to systematize these insights into a true methodology.

Jonah understood that at the heart of every viral piece of content was an emotional response. Data alone could not make something viral. Virality was emotional, not mechanical.

At BuzzFeed, he encouraged his teams to focus obsessively on emotions. Content had to make people feel something strong enough that they would be compelled to share it. Humor, nostalgia, awe, anger, and delight were the primary currencies. He categorized emotions into two buckets: positive high-arousal emotions (like amusement and admiration) and negative high-arousal emotions (like anger and outrage). Both could drive sharing, but Jonah preferred the positive triggers for building long-term trust and goodwill.

One internal BuzzFeed presentation in 2011 laid out the formula starkly: content needed to trigger at least one of three" reactions—"This is me," "This is so true," or

"This is hilarious." Pieces that succeeded on two or all three fronts had an exponentially higher chance of going viral.

Lists became one of BuzzFeed's most potent formats because they inherently invited emotional resonance. They provided structure, predictability, and often a sense of identity. A list titled "21 Signs You Grew Up in the '90s" didn't just deliver nostalgic memories; it created a moment of personal validation for those who lived through that era.

Jonah's other critical innovation was treating content creation as an iterative, scientific process. BuzzFeed was one of the first media companies to integrate rigorous A/B testing into editorial work.

Every headline, every image, and every piece of shared text was a variable that could be tested and optimized. BuzzFeed engineers built internal tools that allowed editors to publish multiple headline versions for the same article, measuring which ones produced higher clickthrough rates and shares. Over time, these experiments generated enormous datasets about what kinds of language, images, and emotional appeals performed best.

For instance, BuzzFeed discovered that specificity often boosted sharing. A headline like "23 Things Only People from Texas Understand" would outperform a vaguer alternative like "Things Texans Know." Jonah's teams learned that numbers in headlines — particularly odd numbers like 17, 23, or 31 — subtly outperformed even numbers. This wasn't theory; it was statistical fact, drawn from millions of data points.

BuzzFeed's CMS, known internally as Hive, was designed not just for publishing, but for experimentation. Editors could monitor real-time traffic and share metrics, adjusting their strategies on the fly. Under Jonah's leadership, creativity and data science weren't separate departments — they were fused at the atomic level of daily operations.

Jonah often spoke about the "viral coefficient"—a" measure of how effectively content propagated through a network. If each person who saw a piece of content shared it with more than one new person, the content would spread exponentially. If the coefficient was less than one, the spread would eventually stall.

At BuzzFeed, editors were trained to think about the viral coefficient as an editorial metric, not just an engineering one. Content wasn't judged solely on traffic but on its inherent shareability. A high-performing post could be one that reached relatively few people initially but had a high viral coefficient, ensuring it would eventually snowball.

Jonah's understanding of the viral coefficient allowed BuzzFeed to engineer "slow burns" as well as "fast flames." Some content was designed for immediate mass sharing, like a timely meme about a breaking news event. Other pieces, like deep nostalgia lists or evergreen quizzes, were crafted to maintain a steady flow of shares over months or even years.

In 2014, BuzzFeed calculated that a significant portion of its overall traffic was driven by content more than 30 days old — a striking contrast to the typical news cycle. Jonah's viral science wasn't just about flash-in-the-pan hits; it was about building a durable reservoir of highly shareable content.

Another major insight Jonah operationalized at BuzzFeed was the concept of "identity content." This was material people shared because it said something about who they were, what they loved, or where they came from.

In 2013, BuzzFeed began producing hyper-targeted pieces like "27 Things Only Introverts Will Understand" or "19 Signs You're Totally a Dog Person." These articles didn't just entertain; they allowed users to announce facets of their personality to their social networks.

Quizzes became an even sharper instrument for this purpose. BuzzFeed's "Which Disney Princess Are You?" quiz, launched in January 2014, quickly became one of the most viral pieces of content in internet history.

Within days, it racked up millions of shares and responses.

He saw quizzes not as mere distractions but as sophisticated identity tools. By encouraging people to categorize themselves ("I'm a Belle!" "I'm a Ravenclaw!"), BuzzFeed created a loop of engagement and sharing that was almost impossible to resist.

Another fundamental part of Jonah's viral mastery was his refusal to treat all platforms the same. Each social network had its own culture, conventions, and sharing mechanics. His teams studied these differences with almost anthropological rigor.

On Facebook, emotional storytelling paired with strong visuals performed best. On Twitter, concise wit and timely commentary were king. On YouTube, storytelling arcs and personality-driven content reigned supreme. On Instagram, aesthetics and aspirational visuals were critical. Jonah insisted that BuzzFeed tailor content specifically for the native strengths of each platform, rather than taking a one-size-fits-all approach.

This mindset led BuzzFeed to thrive across multiple platforms simultaneously — a rare feat at the time. By 2015, BuzzFeed was generating billions of video views per month across Facebook and YouTube while still maintaining strong performance on its owned-and-operated website.

Jonah's platform-native thinking also informed BuzzFeed's decision to invest heavily in new distribution channels early. When Snapchat launched Discover in January 2015, BuzzFeed was one of the first partners. It treated Snapchat not as a secondary outlet, but as a full-fledged content destination, building original teams to create native video, animation, and text pieces for the platform.

One of the most difficult balances Jonah managed was maintaining BuzzFeed's brand integrity while optimizing for virality. He was acutely aware of the risks of pandering, clickbait, and sensationalism. He also understood that viral success could not come at the expense of trust.

BuzzFeed developed internal editorial standards to ensure that even its lightest content met certain thresholds of accuracy and respectfulness. He rejected the idea that going viral required lowering standards. He believed that audiences were sophisticated — that they would reward brands that respected their intelligence and emotional nuance.

In 2016, BuzzFeed faced controversy over its decision to publish the Steele Dossier during the early days of the Trump presidency. Critics accused the company of irresponsibility. Jonah stood by the decision, framing it as a commitment to transparency and public accountability. It was a moment that illustrated the tension between BuzzFeed's viral instincts and its growing journalistic ambitions — a tension he navigated with considerable skill.

By the late 2010s, Jonah's methods had been codified into a formal internal framework known as "cultural cartography." BuzzFeed teams mapped audience interests, emotional triggers, and platform behaviors into detailed charts and profiles. Content creation was informed by this map but never reduced to formulaic templates.

He understood that the science of virality could inform creativity, but not replace it. The best content still required human imagination, storytelling craft, and a deep sense of timing and context. Data could suggest opportunities; it could not manufacture magic.

In speeches and interviews during this period, Jonah often quoted William Gibson's famous line: "The future is already here — it's just not very evenly distributed." His mission was to build a company that lived fully in the future of media — a future shaped by sharing, by identity, by emotion, and by the complex, often unpredictable physics of human connection.

By the early 2020s, Jonah's vision of viral media had been widely imitated but rarely equaled. Every major publisher had adopted some version of BuzzFeed's strategies: emotional storytelling, data-informed headline testing, platform-native distribution, and identity-driven content.

Yet BuzzFeed's early advantages — its integrated tech stack, its disciplined culture of experimentation, and its unwavering focus on human emotions — remained difficult to replicate.

Jonah's mastery of virality had not only built one of the most influential media companies of the digital age. It had reshaped the very grammar of the internet itself.

What spread was not random. What caught fire was not accidental.

It was engineered — by understanding people better than anyone else.

And Jonah Peretti, more than any other figure of his era, had turned that understanding into an empire.

CHAPTER 6: NAVIGATING THE BUZZFEED BOOM AND CHALLENGES

When Jonah Peretti founded BuzzFeed in November 2006, it was a small experimental project tucked away inside a modest corner of New York's tech world. By the middle of the 2010s, it had ballooned into a digital juggernaut with hundreds of employees, a sprawling content empire, and influence that rivaled traditional media giants. Yet, as BuzzFeed soared to unimaginable heights, it also entered a new and turbulent era — one where success carried heavy new expectations, fierce competition, financial volatility, and existential questions about the future of digital media itself.

Jonah's ability to build was undeniable. But his ability to adapt would prove just as essential.

BuzzFeed's acceleration between 2012 and 2016 was extraordinary. The company transformed from a quirky side project into a media powerhouse that shaped conversations across the internet. BuzzFeed had cracked the code of social sharing when most legacy outlets were still obsessed with homepage traffic and SEO.

Investment flowed in accordingly. In 2013, BuzzFeed secured $19.3 million in Series D funding, led by New Enterprise Associates. In August 2014, the company made headlines by raising an additional $50 million from the prestigious venture capital firm Andreessen Horowitz, at a reported valuation of $850 million. That year, BuzzFeed expanded aggressively, opening news bureaus internationally, launching video production at an unprecedented scale, and building its in-house creative agency, BuzzFeed Creative, to capitalize on branded content opportunities.

BuzzFeed Motion Pictures, launched in 2014 under the leadership of Ze Frank and overseen by Jonah, was another major pillar of growth. Housed in a sprawling 250,000-square-foot Los Angeles facility known as "BuzzFeed Studios," the division was producing hundreds of pieces of video content per week, from short skits to experimental series and documentary-style features. Jonah envisioned BuzzFeed not just as a media company, but as the first true modern studio — platform-agnostic, social-first, and built for the on-demand generation.

At the company's peak around 2016, BuzzFeed was reaching over 500 million people monthly across all its properties and platforms. It has become a defining force in viral culture, not just reflecting the internet's obsessions but actively shaping them.

Yet even as BuzzFeed scaled at an astonishing pace, financial pressures were mounting beneath the surface. Venture capital had raised expectations sky-high. Investors were betting that BuzzFeed could become the next Disney or Time Warner for the digital era. Monetization is needed to keep pace with viral reach.

BuzzFeed had initially eschewed traditional banner advertising, focusing instead on native advertising — custom branded content that matched the look and feel of its editorial voice. This worked brilliantly at first. Major brands flocked to BuzzFeed, eager to reach millennial and Gen Z audiences through clever, shareable campaigns.

However, as Facebook tightened its News Feed algorithms beginning in 2015, organic reach for publishers started to decline sharply. Traffic that once flowed freely from social media began to dry up. Branded content, once a money machine, became harder to scale profitably.

BuzzFeed's internal financial goals reflected this growing tension. In 2015, the company had projected revenue of $250 million, but by the end of the year, it reportedly fell short of that target, bringing in closer to $170–$180 million. These figures were never publicly confirmed by BuzzFeed, but internal leaks and industry reporting painted a clear picture: expectations were colliding with the cold realities of monetizing digital audiences.

The collapse of easy Facebook traffic exposed a harsh truth: viral reach alone did not guarantee sustainable profits.

Facing these headwinds, Jonah and his leadership team pursued aggressive diversification strategies.

One major initiative was pivoting toward e-commerce and product revenue. BuzzFeed launched brands like "Tasty"—a" food-focused vertical that exploded in popularity through short recipe videos. By 2016, Tasty's Facebook page had amassed tens of millions of followers, and its videos regularly pulled in hundreds of millions of views.

Recognizing the commercial potential, BuzzFeed expanded Tasty into a full-fledged brand, producing cookbooks, licensing kitchen gadgets, and partnering with retailers like Walmart to sell Tasty-branded cookware. E-commerce became a critical revenue stream, but it required new operational competencies — manufacturing, logistics, and inventory management — far removed from BuzzFeed's original DNA.

Meanwhile, BuzzFeed News, launched officially as a standalone division in 2012 under editor-in-chief Ben Smith, became a formidable journalistic force. Its investigations, particularly around politics, corruption, and technology, earned prestigious accolades, including a Pulitzer Prize finalist nomination in 2018.

Jonah supported the growth of serious journalism at BuzzFeed, seeing it as essential for long-term credibility. But investigative reporting was expensive and slow to monetize. Balancing the costs of a serious newsroom against the demands of venture capital-scale returns created persistent internal tensions.

The internet that BuzzFeed had mastered in the early 2010s was changing rapidly by the second half of the decade. New competitors emerged. Audience habits shifted toward closed messaging platforms and fragmented micro-communities. Facebook pivoted away from news. TikTok's meteoric rise after 2018 rewrote the rules of content discovery and virality yet again.

BuzzFeed's core social distribution strategy — creating content designed to be shared across open networks — was being squeezed from all sides.

Jonah responded by pushing BuzzFeed to become more self-sufficient. He encouraged a greater focus on direct traffic, email newsletters, original commerce products, and subscription services. BuzzFeed's acquisition of HuffPost in November 2020, completed in a deal with Verizon Media, reflected this shift. He hoped to consolidate scale, diversify traffic sources, and deepen engagement with loyal audiences rather than relying solely on volatile social algorithms.

Yet each move came with trade-offs. Scaling subscription revenue was slow and difficult in a crowded media landscape. E-commerce, while promising, faced logistical challenges exacerbated by the global supply chain disruptions of the COVID-19 pandemic. Even as BuzzFeed innovated, profitability remained an elusive goal.

BuzzFeed's meteoric early success had created a vibrant, idealistic internal culture. Employees were passionate about the company's mission to entertain, inform, and connect the world. Many had joined BuzzFeed during its rocket-ship years and expected continuous growth and opportunity.

When financial pressures forced hard decisions, the internal fallout was painful. In January 2019, BuzzFeed laid off approximately 15% of its workforce — around 220 employees — across multiple departments, including BuzzFeed News. Jonah framed the layoffs as necessary to position the company for long-term sustainability. "We have always had the same philosophy," he wrote in a company-wide memo. "We strive to create a great work environment that supports our culture, our values, and our people."

Still, the cuts shook morale. For many employees, it marked the end of an era. BuzzFeed was no longer the carefree viral playground of the early 2010s. It was now a company navigating the hard, often unforgiving realities of media economics.

The layoffs also prompted broader industry soul-searching about the future of digital journalism. BuzzFeed has been one of the great success stories. If even it could not sustain its growth indefinitely, what hope did smaller outlets have?

In a bold move to secure long-term capital and fuel future growth, BuzzFeed announced in June 2021 that it would go public through a merger with a special purpose acquisition company (SPAC), 890 Fifth Avenue Partners. The deal valued BuzzFeed at approximately $1.5 billion and was positioned as a way to give BuzzFeed the resources needed to expand its commerce, content, and ad businesses.

However, the SPAC route proved fraught with challenges. BuzzFeed's stock debuted on the Nasdaq under the ticker symbol BZFD in December 2021, but the rollout was rocky. Shares fell sharply in the days after the listing, and a significant number of SPAC investors opted to redeem their shares before the merger closed, reducing the cash BuzzFeed actually received.

The public markets exposed BuzzFeed to new pressures: quarterly earnings expectations, shareholder scrutiny, and short-term volatility. Jonah now had to manage not just the company's operational health but also its public valuation — a different and often less predictable battlefield.

Despite the difficult debut, Jonah remained publicly optimistic. He continued to articulate a vision of BuzzFeed as a diversified, multi-platform media company capable of thriving in a post-social era. Yet privately, the challenges were undeniable. The road ahead would be steeper than at any point in BuzzFeed's history.

Through all of this turbulence, Jonah himself evolved. Once known as a quirky, hoodie-wearing technologist who delighted in internet memes, he had grown into a seasoned, if sometimes reluctant, CEO navigating the complex realities of running a large, public company.

His leadership style remained analytical and iterative. He remained committed to experimentation, to learning from data, and to thinking several moves ahead. But he also became more visibly attuned to the emotional realities of leading through uncertainty. In public statements and interviews after 2020, he spoke more often about resilience, adaptation, and the human costs of disruption.

Jonah had always understood virality. Now he understood endurance.

As BuzzFeed moved through the 2020s, it stood at a crossroads. The company's brand was still powerful, its reach still immense. Its experiments in commerce, production, and subscriptions held promise. Yet the broader landscape remained unforgiving. Digital media's economics were fundamentally more brutal than they had been when Jonah first started tinkering with viral content at the MIT Media Lab in the early 2000s.

Jonah's genius had always been in seeing patterns before others did — in understanding not just what the internet was, but what it was becoming. Whether he could guide BuzzFeed successfully into its next chapter would depend on more than just understanding virality. It would require building resilience into the company's DNA.

The BuzzFeed boom was real. The challenges were realer still.

And Jonah Peretti, for better or worse, remained at the center of the storm he had helped create.

CHAPTER 7: BUZZFEED NEWS: JOURNALISM IN THE DIGITAL AGE

When Jonah Peretti launched BuzzFeed News as an official division in 2012, it was not a predictable move. At that time, BuzzFeed was best known for its viral quizzes, humorous listicles, and internet memes. Serious journalism seemed almost antithetical to the brand's DNA. Yet he believed that building credibility in hard news was essential not only to BuzzFeed's future, but to the broader project of defining what news could be in a digital-first era.

He envisioned a newsroom that embraced the best parts of internet culture — speed, relatability, and shareability — while refusing to compromise on the fundamental values of journalistic rigor: accuracy, fairness, depth, and accountability.

The gamble was audacious. The results would be transformative, both for BuzzFeed and for digital journalism as a whole.

BuzzFeed News officially took shape under the leadership of Ben Smith, whom Jonah recruited as editor-in-chief in December 2011. Smith was a high-profile political reporter at Politico at the time, respected for his sharp instincts and deep sources. Bringing him aboard signaled that BuzzFeed News would be more than just a side project.

Smith was given wide latitude to build the newsroom he envisioned. Early hires reflected a mix of traditional reporters and digital natives, people who understood both shoe-leather reporting and the rhythms of the internet. The aim was clear: produce original, high-impact journalism that would be widely read and shared.

By 2013, BuzzFeed News had reporters based in Washington, D.C., New York, Los Angeles, and London. Its political coverage, particularly during the 2012 U.S.

presidential election, began earning respect. Stories were fast, sharp, and often beat traditional outlets on emerging narratives.

BuzzFeed News did not try to mimic The New York Times or The Washington Post. Instead, it cultivated a tone that was direct, informal when appropriate, and aimed at making complex issues accessible without dumbing them down. Jonah encouraged this stylistic innovation, believing that the future of journalism lay in combining substance with approachability.

BuzzFeed News truly came into its own with its groundbreaking investigative work. Throughout the mid-2010s, the newsroom tackled subjects that few expected from a company better known for "Which Disney Princess Are You?" quizzes.

One of the earliest signs of its investigative muscle came in 2014, when BuzzFeed News published a major series on sexual assault allegations against universities, focusing on mishandled cases and systemic failures to protect victims. Reporters like Katie J.M. Baker produced deeply reported, empathetic stories that sparked national conversations about Title IX enforcement.

In 2015, BuzzFeed News made headlines again when it published a major investigation into the Islamic State's funding operations, based on leaked documents and extensive interviews. The reporting was praised for its depth, context, and refusal to sensationalize complex geopolitics.

Perhaps most notably, BuzzFeed News distinguished itself through its dogged reporting on Russian disinformation and interference in U.S. politics. During and after the 2016 U.S. presidential election, BuzzFeed reporters, including Anthony Cormier and Jason Leopold, pursued stories about foreign influence operations, campaign finance violations, and political corruption with tenacity that rivaled any major outlet.

In January 2017, BuzzFeed News made a controversial decision that would become a defining moment: it published the full Steele dossier — a collection of memos compiled by former British intelligence officer Christopher Steele alleging connections between Donald Trump's campaign and Russia. Other media organizations, including CNN, had reported on the existence of the dossier but had refrained from publishing it in full.

Jonah and Ben Smith defended the decision as a commitment to transparency. They argued that the dossier was already being circulated among politicians, journalists, and law enforcement, and that the public had a right to see it and assess it for themselves. Critics accused BuzzFeed of irresponsibility, arguing that the dossier contained unverified and salacious claims. Supporters praised the boldness of the move, seeing it as a refusal to shield powerful institutions from public scrutiny.

The decision ignited fierce debate about the role of media in the digital age — whether platforms like BuzzFeed News should act as gatekeepers or open conduits for information. Jonah Peretti remained steadfast that BuzzFeed's responsibility was to empower audiences with access to primary sources, even when the material was uncomfortable.

Despite skepticism from some quarters, BuzzFeed News's commitment to serious journalism earned growing recognition.

In 2017, BuzzFeed News was a finalist for the Pulitzer Prize in International Reporting for a series on how officials in Mexico systematically covered up extrajudicial killings. The series, led by reporters Karla Zabludovsky and others, uncovered chilling evidence of state complicity in human rights abuses, documented through on-the-ground reporting and leaked internal documents.

In 2018, BuzzFeed News again became a Pulitzer finalist, this time for International Reporting, for its investigation into a global campaign of assassination targeting political opponents and dissidents. These recognitions, from journalism's highest body, affirmed what Jonah had bet on from the beginning: that digital-first journalism could meet the highest standards of the profession.

BuzzFeed News reporters also won National Magazine Awards, George Polk Awards, and other honors for investigative work across topics ranging from systemic racism in law enforcement to abuses in private foster care systems.

While BuzzFeed News grew into a formidable journalistic institution, it remained part of a broader company built on viral content and entertainment. Balancing these two identities was not always easy.

BuzzFeed's main homepage, designed to surface the most popular content at any given time, often featured a mix of serious investigations alongside light-hearted quizzes, memes, and celebrity gossip. Some critics argued that this mixture diluted the impact of BuzzFeed News's serious work, making it harder for audiences to distinguish between journalism and entertainment.

Jonah acknowledged the tension but insisted it was not a flaw — it was the point. He believed that modern audiences could move fluidly between moods and interests and that serious journalism did not need to be cloaked in solemnity to be powerful. A site that celebrated both Taylor Swift memes and human rights reporting was, in Jonah's view, a more accurate reflection of the totality of human curiosity.

Still, internally, there were tensions. Some BuzzFeed News journalists chafed at being under the same umbrella as viral content creators. Efforts were made to more clearly brand BuzzFeed News separately, including distinct social media accounts, design elements, and homepages focused exclusively on news content.

In 2018, BuzzFeed News officially began operating under its own dedicated domain, buzzfeednews.com, further cementing its independence within the larger BuzzFeed ecosystem.

One of the enduring challenges Jonah faced was the economics of serious journalism.

Investigative reporting is expensive, time-consuming, and does not easily lend itself to the advertising or sponsored content models that sustained the rest of BuzzFeed. Unlike a viral Tasty video or a quiz shared millions of times, a deeply reported story might take months to produce and might reach a comparatively small, though highly engaged, audience.

BuzzFeed News pursued various strategies to address this tension. It experimented with a membership program in 2018, asking loyal audiences to contribute financially to support investigative work. Early signs were promising, but converting viral traffic into paying members proved more difficult than hoped.

Additionally, the pressures of a broader advertising downturn — accelerated by Facebook's algorithm changes and the COVID-19 pandemic's economic fallout — hit BuzzFeed News especially hard. In 2020, BuzzFeed News underwent significant restructuring, including the elimination of entire international news desks in the UK and Australia.

Throughout these challenges, Jonah remained committed to preserving BuzzFeed News's core mission. He resisted calls to shutter the division entirely, even when doing so might have made short-term financial sense. To Jonah, having a credible journalistic institution was not a luxury; it was essential to BuzzFeed's identity and long-term credibility.

In March 2023, BuzzFeed announced a significant shift. BuzzFeed News would be shutting down as an independent operation. The move was part of a broader cost-cutting effort amid a difficult advertising market and broader economic downturn.

Jonah framed the decision not as a repudiation of journalism but as a necessary pivot. He emphasized that BuzzFeed would continue producing news through HuffPost, which remained profitable and sustainable under BuzzFeed's ownership.

The closure of BuzzFeed News marked the end of one of the most ambitious experiments in digital journalism history. It underscored the brutal financial realities facing even the most innovative newsrooms. Yet it also affirmed the profound impact BuzzFeed News had during its decade-long existence.

His gamble had reshaped the expectations of what digital journalism could be. It had produced award-winning investigations, broken major stories, and helped usher a generation of journalists into the profession.

The experiment ended, but the influence remained.

BuzzFeed News left an indelible mark on journalism.

It proved that serious reporting could emerge from unexpected places. It showed that internet-native media companies could produce work as rigorous, impactful, and consequential as any traditional outlet. It trained hundreds of journalists who went on to leadership roles at The New York Times, The Washington Post, and other legacy institutions.

Most importantly, BuzzFeed News forced the journalism industry to rethink its assumptions. It challenged the idea that "real" news could only be produced in a certain format or tone. It demonstrated that audiences cared about good reporting, even if they discovered it in the same feed as memes and listicles.

Jonah Peretti's commitment to building a serious newsroom, against the grain of skepticism and financial headwinds, remains one of his most enduring contributions to media history.

In a world where information flows faster and more chaotically than ever, the lessons of BuzzFeed News — about transparency, accessibility, rigor, and innovation — will continue to reverberate for years to come.

CHAPTER 8: AI AND THE FUTURE OF MEDIA

Jonah Peretti has never been one to simply follow technological trends. Throughout his career, he has consistently positioned himself at the intersection of culture and innovation, anticipating shifts that would redefine how content is created, distributed, and consumed. His latest and most ambitious pivot centers around artificial intelligence — a development that he sees not just as another tool but as a transformative force that will shape the next era of media.

The decision to integrate AI into BuzzFeed's operations was not abrupt. It was the product of years of studying emerging technologies and a recognition that the old models of digital publishing — reliant on viral traffic, social media referrals, and banner ads — were crumbling under the weight of algorithmic unpredictability and changing consumer behavior.

In January 2023, Jonah made headlines when he publicly announced that BuzzFeed would begin using AI to assist in content creation, starting with quizzes and expanding into other creative areas. The move was immediately controversial, heralded by some as forward-thinking and criticized by others as a threat to human creativity and journalistic integrity.

But for Jonah, it was a logical step rooted in the same principle that had guided his work since his MIT Media Lab days: embrace new tools to better serve human curiosity, imagination, and storytelling.

BuzzFeed's first large-scale AI initiative launched in February 2023, focusing on one of its signature content formats — quizzes. Partnering with OpenAI's technology, BuzzFeed developed a system it called "Infinity Quizzes," which allowed users to input personalized details and receive individualized results generated dynamically by AI.

Unlike traditional quizzes, which relied on pre-written questions and a fixed set of outcomes, Infinity Quizzes created unique narratives for each participant based on their choices. For example, a user taking a quiz like "Design Your Dream Vacation and We'll Write a Romantic Comedy About It" would not simply get assigned one of a dozen preset results. Instead, the AI would craft a short story tailored to the user's specific preferences.

This approach fits perfectly with BuzzFeed's brand — playful, interactive, and deeply personal. It also addressed a long-standing challenge: how to create an infinite amount of content without an infinite editorial staff.

He made clear that AI was not replacing human creativity. Instead, it was enhancing it. Editors and writers still conceived the themes, designed the templates, and curated the prompts. AI filled in the variable details, offering a new level of scale and personalization that would have been impossible manually.

The early reception was mixed but largely positive. Audience engagement with AI-powered quizzes was strong, and BuzzFeed began quietly experimenting with AI-generated elements in other areas, including short-form content for BuzzFeed's Tasty food brand and lifestyle sections.

Jonah Peretti articulated his broader AI strategy during BuzzFeed's Q4 2022 earnings call, held in March 2023. He told investors that he envisioned a future where AI worked alongside human creators to produce content that was more dynamic, personalized, and cost-effective.

In a memo to staff dated January 26, 2023, Jonah wrote:

> "In 2023, you'll see AI-inspired content move from an R&D stage to part of our core business, enhancing the quiz experience, informing our brainstorming, and personalizing our content for our audience."

Importantly, Jonah did not describe AI as replacing journalists, editors, or creators. Rather, he saw AI as a partner — a creative collaborator that could handle repetitive tasks, generate first drafts for refinement, offer new ideas, and unlock new types of storytelling.

He stressed that BuzzFeed's value proposition remained rooted in human authenticity: the humor, empathy, insight, and cultural fluency that algorithms could not replicate. AI would make human creativity more efficient, not obsolete.

This philosophy stood in contrast to more dystopian visions of AI-dominated media, positioning him once again as an optimist about technology's role in culture.

By mid-2023, BuzzFeed had expanded its use of AI beyond quizzes.

One major initiative involved AI-assisted brainstorming for listicles and video concepts. Editors used AI tools to generate potential topics, headlines, and formats, which human creators then vetted and refined. This sped up the ideation process and allowed BuzzFeed to experiment with a broader range of content formats without overburdening its creative teams.

BuzzFeed also began integrating AI into visual content creation. Working with AI art generation tools, BuzzFeed designers produced custom illustrations and images for articles, social media posts, and branded content campaigns. AI-assisted visual production reduced costs and turnaround times while offering fresh aesthetic possibilities.

In September 2023, BuzzFeed launched a pilot program using AI to help generate first drafts of product reviews and recommendation lists for its shopping section. Human editors were still responsible for fact-checking, refining language, and ensuring that the final pieces met BuzzFeed's editorial standards. However, the AI-generated drafts helped overcome bottlenecks in content volume, allowing BuzzFeed to capture more search traffic and affiliate revenue opportunities.

BuzzFeed also entered partnerships with emerging AI companies, including collaborations with startups developing text-to-video and synthetic media technologies. While these initiatives were experimental, they reflected his long-term belief that AI would revolutionize not just written content, but video, audio, and interactive formats as well.

Despite Jonah's careful framing, BuzzFeed's embrace of AI was not universally welcomed.

Many critics worried that AI-generated content would flood the internet with low-quality material, contribute to misinformation, or displace human workers. Others raised ethical concerns about transparency — whether audiences would know when content was partially or fully AI-generated.

BuzzFeed took steps to address these concerns. Jonah mandated that all AI-assisted content must be transparently labeled. He emphasized that no news reporting at BuzzFeed News — while it still operated — would be AI-generated, preserving a firewall between creative entertainment content and serious journalism.

Nevertheless, skepticism persisted. Industry observers questioned whether audiences would trust AI-assisted content. Some advertisers expressed caution, wary of potential backlash against synthetic media.

He acknowledged these risks but remained bullish. He argued that responsible, transparent use of AI could build trust, not erode it. He believed that the real threat to media was not AI itself, but companies that used it recklessly or deceptively.

In a public interview with The New York Times at the DealBook Summit in November 2023, Jonah stated:

> "Every major technological leap has been met with fear and misunderstanding. What matters is how you use the tools — whether you use them to create more meaningful connections, or to undermine trust. At BuzzFeed, we're choosing the former."

Part of Jonah's urgency around AI stemmed from economic necessity.

BuzzFeed, like most digital media companies, faced ongoing financial headwinds. Facebook's reduced referral traffic, Google's algorithm changes, the rise of

TikTok, and broader shifts in advertiser spending all undermined traditional revenue streams.

BuzzFeed's Q1 2023 earnings report, released in May 2023, showed a 27% year-over-year decline in overall revenue, with advertising down significantly. Commerce and licensing offered some growth, but not enough to offset the losses.

AI, in Jonah's vision, offered a path to sustainability. By using AI to create more content at lower marginal costs, BuzzFeed could protect its margins even amid declining CPMs and unpredictable social traffic. It could also offer advertisers new, personalized campaign formats driven by AI insights.

In December 2023, BuzzFeed announced the launch of "BuzzFeed AI Studios," a dedicated division focused on building AI-driven content products for brand partners. The initiative aimed to create customized interactive content — quizzes, games, story generators — tailored to specific brand narratives.

Early clients included major CPG and entertainment brands, and initial campaigns showed strong engagement metrics. Jonah saw this as proof that AI-driven creativity could not only sustain BuzzFeed but also offer new premium revenue streams.

As of early 2025, Jonah Peretti's vision for AI and media remains expansive.

He believes that the future of digital content lies in hyper-personalization: media experiences tailored to individual users based on their preferences, histories, and moods. AI is the engine that will make this possible.

He envisions AI-generated news briefs customized to a user's interests, AI-assisted learning tools that make complex topics accessible, and AI-driven entertainment that creates unique stories for every audience member. BuzzFeed's role, in his mind, is not to replace human creativity but to supercharge it — to build platforms where people feel more seen, understood, and engaged.

Jonah also sees potential for AI to help bridge cultural gaps. By enabling faster translation, cultural adaptation, and personalization, AI could allow media companies to reach truly global audiences without losing nuance or authenticity.

Yet he remains aware of the ethical minefields. He has called for industry-wide standards around transparency, disclosure, and accountability in AI content creation. He has argued that companies must prioritize quality over quantity, trust over virality, and human values over technological novelty.

BuzzFeed's embrace of AI, under Jonah's leadership, has already influenced the broader media industry.

Legacy outlets like The New York Times, The Washington Post, and CNN have begun experimenting cautiously with AI tools. New startups have emerged offering AI-driven journalism, AI-generated entertainment, and AI-enhanced marketing services. Venture capital has poured into synthetic media, recognizing the disruptive potential.

Yet few have gone as far or as publicly as BuzzFeed. Jonah's willingness to move early, experiment openly, and articulate a coherent ethical framework has made him a central figure in debates about AI's role in media.

Whether or not every bet succeeds, Jonah Peretti's integration of AI into BuzzFeed's operations represents a defining moment in the evolution of digital publishing — one that future historians will study as a pivotal shift in how humanity creates, shares, and experiences stories.

The media landscape is changing faster than ever. He is not trying to preserve the past. He is building for the next reality.

And, as has been true throughout his career, he is doing so not by rejecting the future, but by running toward it — with imagination, optimism, and a relentless belief in the power of creativity and connection.

CHAPTER 9: SHAPING INTERNET CULTURE

Jonah Peretti's imprint on the fabric of internet culture is profound, wide-reaching, and still evolving. Unlike many digital entrepreneurs who aimed only to profit from the internet's growth, Jonah instinctively understood the web as a cultural phenomenon — a living, breathing ecosystem driven by humor, curiosity, outrage, and, above all, participation.

From his early experiments with viral content to the expansive influence of BuzzFeed's sprawling network, he has played a central role in molding the memes, challenges, and interaction patterns that now define online life. His contribution to shaping internet culture is not merely incidental; it is foundational.

Jonah's influence on the cultural DNA of the internet traces back to the Nike Sweatshop Email incident of 2001. While most people at the time saw the internet as a platform for information or commerce, Jonah recognized its potential as a medium for satire, activism, and viral storytelling.

By engaging Nike in a public email exchange over customized shoes emblazoned with the word "sweatshop," Jonah tapped into an emerging dynamic: internet users' hunger for witty, pointed content they could share with their social networks. His emails circulated not just because they were funny, but because they allowed people to feel like participants in a broader social critique.

This model — using humor and controversy to galvanize conversation — became a blueprint for much of what internet culture would later become.

Following the Nike exchange, Jonah co-founded ReBlog in 2003, alongside Eyebeam colleague Alexander Galloway. ReBlog was a groundbreaking content aggregation platform that allowed users to curate and republish material from across the web. Though it operated on a small scale, ReBlog introduced ideas that would become central to the viral economy: curation, aggregation, and the elevation of user voice.

These early projects revealed Jonah's core insight: virality was not just about attention. It was about participation. People didn't just want to consume content; they wanted to feel like they were part of it, shaping and sharing it within their communities.

When Jonah co-founded The Huffington Post in May 2005 alongside Arianna Huffington, Kenneth Lerer, and Andrew Breitbart, he embedded participatory dynamics into its DNA. Unlike traditional news outlets, HuffPost invited unpaid bloggers, amateur writers, and celebrities to contribute content directly to the platform.

This approach democratized publishing and blurred the line between professional and amateur, creating a model where news and commentary circulated socially as much as editorially. In many ways, HuffPost anticipated the later explosion of social media-driven discourse — memes, takes, and viral debates that now dominate online life.

His background in viral ideas made him particularly effective at architecting HuffPost's content strategy. He understood how to frame headlines for maximum social sharing and how to surface provocative or humorous angles that would spark conversations across early platforms like MySpace and, increasingly, Facebook.

HuffPost's meteoric rise was not just a business success; it was a cultural shift. It signaled that the gatekeepers of traditional media were losing control and that participatory, shareable content was the future.

When Jonah founded BuzzFeed in November 2006, he sharpened his focus even further. BuzzFeed's original purpose was to track what content was going viral on the internet — a kind of cultural seismograph. But Jonah soon realized he could do more than observe trends; he could create them.

BuzzFeed's early success came from mastering the micro-formats that fueled social sharing: listicles, quizzes, reaction GIFs, and short, emotionally resonant articles. Each format wasn't just engineered for clicks; it was designed for participation. Jonah's team developed content that people would want to share because it expressed something about their identity, their humor, or their values.

Formats like

- "21 Things Only True '90s Kids Will Understand"
- "Which Disney Princess Are You?"
- "27 Problems Only Tall People Will Understand"

These pieces weren't merely entertainment; they were social artifacts. Sharing them allowed users to signal group identity, nostalgia, aspirations, and humor.

BuzzFeed's viral successes created some of the internet's most iconic early memes and tropes. The platform didn't just reflect internet culture — it actively shaped it, creating templates that other publishers, marketers, and even individual users would replicate across social media platforms.

Perhaps nowhere was Jonah's influence more visible than in the meme economy.

BuzzFeed helped popularize reaction memes, listicle memes, and participatory challenges long before they became mainstream. Their lightweight, low-barrier-to-entry nature encourages mass participation. In essence, BuzzFeed turned internet culture into a playground where anyone could join, remix, and amplify trends.

One landmark example is the rise of reaction GIFs. Around 2012-2013, BuzzFeed heavily invested in cataloging and curating GIFs that users could deploy in their own conversations. By organizing GIFs by emotion—"when" you're feeling sassy," "when you need to shut someone down," "when bae texts" you"—BuzzFeed trained an entire generation to use visual media as a core part of online self-expression.

Later, BuzzFeed's coverage and amplification of viral challenges — from the Harlem Shake in early 2013 to the Ice Bucket Challenge in mid-2014— helped solidify a new mode of internet engagement: participatory virality. Instead of passively consuming a meme, users were invited to perform it themselves, record it, and pass it along.

Jonah instinctively grasped that virality was most powerful when it created a sense of belonging. Challenges allowed people to feel connected to a broader movement, whether it was silly (like the Harlem Shake) or altruistic (like raising money for ALS research).

BuzzFeed's impact on the meme ecosystem was so significant that by 2015, traditional news outlets like CNN and The New York Times began assigning reporters specifically to "internet culture" beats — a tacit admission that memes and viral phenomena were now central to understanding contemporary society.

Jonah Peretti's influence extended beyond content formats to the very structure of online interaction.

BuzzFeed's emphasis on "identity" content"—pieces that said something about who you were ("15 Signs You're a

Total Introvert," "23 Things Only Middle Children" Understand")—fueled a broader shift in how people used the internet. The web was no longer just a place to consume information; it became a primary venue for performing and negotiating personal identity.

By creating content that people saw as extensions of themselves, he accelerated the rise of the personal brand culture that now dominates platforms like Instagram, TikTok, and Twitter.

Moreover, BuzzFeed's close relationship with Facebook shaped the dynamics of content distribution. In 2013, BuzzFeed was one of the first publishers to fully optimize its strategy around Facebook's News Feed, crafting headlines and formats that played perfectly to the platform's sharing algorithms.

This symbiosis influenced not just what people shared but how they interacted. Viral content became less about passive reading and more about emotional resonance, group belonging, and status signaling.

By 2015, BuzzFeed's "Tasty" vertical had similarly redefined video content. Instead of long-form cooking shows, Tasty's viral recipes were quick, visually driven, and designed to be consumed soundlessly — perfectly tuned to the mobile, social-first reality of modern internet life.

These shifts didn't just impact BuzzFeed's traffic. They changed user behavior across the internet, setting expectations for immediacy, visual storytelling, and shareability that now define digital media.

At the core of Jonah Peretti's influence is a consistent belief: the internet is a participatory medium.

Unlike the old broadcast model — where a few spoke and many listened — he saw the web as a place where every user was also a creator, curator, and amplifier. His platforms never treated audiences as passive consumers. They treated them as collaborators.

Even BuzzFeed's most "lightweight" content — quizzes, listicles, memes — were participatory experiences. They invited users to see themselves in the content, to react, to share, and to add their own commentary.

His approach foreshadowed the user-generated content revolutions that later fueled TikTok, Instagram Stories, YouTube Shorts, and other participatory platforms.

While he did not invent these dynamics, he industrialized and popularized them at a scale few others achieved.

Of course, Jonah's impact on internet culture has not been without criticism.

Some critics argue that BuzzFeed and similar platforms contributed to the rise of "listicle culture," encouraging superficiality, clickbait, and a constant churn of low-effort content. Others claim that the relentless pursuit of virality distorted incentives, favoring shock value and emotional manipulation over substance.

He has acknowledged some of these tensions. In various interviews, he has emphasized that virality should not be pursued at the expense of trust, ethics, or quality.

BuzzFeed's investment in serious journalism, particularly with BuzzFeed News from 2012 onward, was partly a corrective effort — a way to demonstrate that viral engagement and substantive reporting could coexist.

Nevertheless, the broader criticisms highlight the immense power — and potential pitfalls — of shaping online culture.

As of 2025, Jonah Peretti's influence on internet culture remains unmistakable.

Even as new platforms and formats emerge, the core dynamics he helped pioneer — participatory content, identity-driven sharing, and lightweight engagement mechanisms — continue to define digital life.

Every viral TikTok challenge, every Instagram meme page, and every Twitter thread that turns into a cultural moment bears traces of the structures he helped build.

His legacy is not just in the companies he founded but in the way billions of people now interact, create, and connect online.

The culture of the internet is a living, evolving entity. But its DNA — participatory, identity-driven, viral — owes an indelible debt to Jonah Peretti's vision, experimentation, and relentless curiosity about what makes people share.

CHAPTER 10: THE PERSONAL SIDE OF JONAH PERETTI

Behind the viral memes, the media empires, and the revolution in internet culture, Jonah Peretti remains a surprisingly private and self-effacing figure. Unlike many founders who eagerly sought the spotlight, Jonah always allowed his work — the platforms he built, the audiences he empowered — to speak louder than his personal brand.

Understanding him beyond his professional accomplishments requires looking closer at his values, his intellectual influences, his creative instincts, and the lifestyle choices he has made outside of building digital giants. His personal ethos shaped not only BuzzFeed and The Huffington Post but also the culture of the modern internet itself.

Born on January 1, 1974, in Oakland, California, Jonah grew up in a family that valued ideas, education, and creativity. His father was an artist and builder, while his mother was a schoolteacher who eventually transitioned into a career in counseling. His upbringing blended practical craftsmanship with intellectual rigor and emotional intelligence, giving him a wide foundation for understanding different ways of engaging with the world.

The Peretti household encouraged free thinking. Conversations around the dinner table often centered around politics, media, and philosophy. Jonah's half-brother, Ben Peretti, and his sister, Chelsea Peretti — who would later become a successful comedian, actress, and writer — shared a household environment where humor and critical inquiry were intertwined.

Chelsea's success in comedy and Jonah's mastery of viral humor both trace back to the same core family culture: a keen awareness of the absurdities of the world, combined with an ability to translate those observations into creative action.

Growing up in the diverse, socially conscious environment of Oakland in the 1980s and early 1990s also had a lasting impact. Jonah developed a deep appreciation for multiculturalism, progressive politics, and the power of communities — ideals that would later shape BuzzFeed's editorial philosophy and workplace culture.

After graduating from high school, Jonah attended the University of California, Santa Cruz, where he majored in environmental studies. His choice reflected his early commitment to progressive causes and his growing interest in systems — ecosystems, social systems, and information systems.

At UCSC, he began developing his habit of blending disciplines that many considered unrelated. He combined environmental science with a fascination for technology, media theory, and participatory democracy.

After earning his undergraduate degree, Jonah pursued a master's degree at the MIT Media Lab, one of the most forward-thinking academic institutions in the world. His time at MIT, from the late 1990s into the early 2000s, was transformative.

At the Media Lab, Jonah was exposed to cutting-edge research in computer science, media arts, and sociology. He studied under Professor Henry Jenkins, a leading thinker on participatory culture and transmedia storytelling. Jonah absorbed Jenkins' ideas about "convergence culture"—the" blending of traditional media with grassroots participatory culture — and those concepts became central to his future ventures.

MIT also nurtured his comfort with experimentation. He saw that small experiments could have outsized impacts in a networked world, a lesson that directly informed his future success with viral content.

More importantly, MIT showed him that it was possible to be both analytical and creative. Data and storytelling, science and art — Jonah rejected the false dichotomy between them, blending them in everything he built thereafter.

Even as BuzzFeed's influence expanded dramatically in the 2010s, Jonah avoided the kind of celebrity entrepreneur lifestyle embraced by peers like Elon Musk or Mark Zuckerberg. He gave a few interviews. He rarely made bombastic public appearances. He maintained an understated personal image that sometimes puzzled those expecting a flamboyant media mogul.

His life has always centered on intellectual curiosity rather than personal fame. His interviews, when he gave them, were often filled with references to academic concepts, internet culture dynamics, and theories of human behavior rather than self-promotion.

Despite being the architect of content that reached billions, he preferred a life that allowed him space to think, experiment, and build without constant public scrutiny.

He once joked in an interview that if BuzzFeed ever created a quiz about him, the result would be, "You're a socially awkward nerd who accidentally built a media empire."

Behind the humor lay a deeper truth: Jonah never sought to dominate the conversation; he sought to understand and shape it.

Jonah's professional choices have reflected a willingness to risk personal security for creative innovation.

When BuzzFeed began investing heavily in original journalism around 2012, Jonah knew the financial risks. Serious investigative reporting was expensive, time-consuming, and didn't always translate into viral traffic. But he believed that building a credible news organization was essential for the long-term health of the internet.

In interviews from 2013 and 2014, Jonah expressed concerns about the "junkification" of online content. He argued that platforms like BuzzFeed had a responsibility to not just chase virality but also invest in quality information that empowered audiences.

This commitment often came at personal cost. BuzzFeed News ran ambitious investigations — from uncovering systemic corruption in local governments to reporting on abuses by global corporations — that made the company political targets. BuzzFeed News' groundbreaking dossier publication about Donald Trump and Russia in January 2017 brought international attention but also intense controversy and legal battles.

Through it all, Jonah maintained his commitment to independent, credible journalism, even as the financial pressures on BuzzFeed mounted. This was not the path of a profit-maximizing CEO obsessed with quarterly results. It was the choice of a builder motivated by principles larger than personal gain.

Despite his immense influence, Jonah has always maintained a relatively low-key personal life. He is married to Andrea Harner, a researcher and blogger known for her witty takes on internet culture and psychology. The couple has two children.

His lifestyle reflects his values: curiosity, humility, family, and a deep belief in the potential of human creativity. He is known to prefer small, intimate gatherings to large industry events. He spends much of his free time reading, reflecting on technological trends, and staying connected to emerging subcultures online.

In rare interviews, he has referenced his love of experimental art, science fiction, and political philosophy. He is particularly interested in how culture evolves through networks — a fascination that permeates everything he has built.

Though he now lives in New York City, Jonah retains a strong connection to his West Coast roots. His early experiences in Oakland's diverse, progressive environment continue to inform his politics, his worldview, and his media philosophy.

He remains deeply optimistic about the internet's potential to empower voices, despite having witnessed firsthand its capacity for distortion and abuse.

At the heart of Jonah's creative drive are several core values:

- **Participation over Consumption**: He believes the internet's highest value lies in its participatory nature. This ethos drove the user-centered strategies of HuffPost and BuzzFeed alike.
- **Inclusivity**: From HuffPost's early open blogging platform to BuzzFeed's identity-driven content, Jonah's work has consistently embraced a wide spectrum of voices.

- **Curiosity and Experimentation**: He sees creativity as a process of constant iteration. His platforms encourage experimentation at every level, from headline testing to new storytelling formats.
- **Humor and Humanity**: Humor has always been central to Jonah's approach, not as a way to trivialize important issues, but as a tool for connection and cultural commentary.
- **Responsibility**: Especially after BuzzFeed News' expansion, Jonah emphasized the need for media companies to take their role in society seriously.

These values not only shaped Jonah's business ventures but also provided a moral compass as he navigated the shifting tides of digital media.

Though Jonah rarely speaks publicly about his political views, his professional actions have consistently supported progressive causes.

BuzzFeed has promoted LGBTQ+ representation, gender equity, and racial diversity across its editorial teams and content. His companies have also supported causes like press freedom, internet neutrality, and human rights, often at times when it would have been easier — and safer — to remain silent.

Jonah's preference for action over rhetoric reflects his broader personal philosophy: change the systems, empower the people, and trust that meaningful culture will follow.

This low-key, principled approach has earned him respect across the industry, even among those who disagreed with BuzzFeed's stylistic approach to news and entertainment.

By 2020, the media landscape had changed dramatically. Social media algorithms shifted. Advertising revenue models faltered. Political polarization intensified. BuzzFeed, like many digital media companies, faced layoffs, restructurings, and difficult transitions.

Through these storms, Jonah remained remarkably steady. His leadership style — thoughtful, experimental, and patient — prioritized long-term survival over short-term optics.

Even when BuzzFeed faced criticism for organizational decisions, he maintained an open dialogue with employees, acknowledging missteps without defensive bluster.

His resilience during these difficult periods speaks to a deeper personal strength: a commitment to purpose that transcends immediate success or failure.

Jonah has never been merely a viral magician. He has been a builder of systems, a believer in participation, and a quiet champion for the creative potential of ordinary people in a networked world.

As of 2025, Jonah Peretti remains one of the most influential yet least publicized figures in modern digital culture.

He is not a bombastic leader with endless keynote speeches or a public provocateur courting controversy. He is, at his core, an experimentalist: a thinker, a tinkerer, and a builder fascinated by how humans connect, communicate, and create meaning together.

His personal life — grounded, humble, intellectually curious — reflects the same principles that have animated his work. For Jonah, the internet was never just a marketplace. It was a canvas, a playground, and a tool for collective invention.

And though trends shift and technologies change, that vision — of a participatory, creative internet — remains as relevant today as it was when Jonah first began his quiet, revolutionary work in the early 2000s.

CONCLUSION

Jonah Peretti's influence on the digital world is not measured simply by the companies he built or the viral moments he engineered. His true legacy lies in how he fundamentally altered the mechanics of communication, storytelling, and media distribution in the 21st century. Few figures have so seamlessly combined an understanding of human psychology, network theory, and creative storytelling into a cohesive vision that reimagined the global media landscape.

Starting from humble roots in Oakland, California, he cultivated a rare blend of curiosity, humor, and discipline. His journey from environmental studies at the University of California, Santa Cruz, to his groundbreaking experiments at the MIT Media Lab during the late 1990s was marked by a commitment to understanding how information spreads, how audiences think, and how culture evolves in real time.

The Nike sweatshop email incident in 2001 was not just an early viral moment; it was a manifestation of Jonah's intuitive grasp of how humor, irony, and moral outrage could combine into powerful internet phenomena. Rather than letting that moment be a one-off novelty, Jonah recognized the underlying patterns at play and devoted his career to harnessing those forces responsibly and creatively.

Co-founding The Huffington Post in 2005 alongside Arianna Huffington, Kenneth Lerer, and Andrew Breitbart, Jonah contributed to the democratization of content creation and distribution. By empowering a broad range of voices through an open blogging platform, HuffPost set the stage for participatory journalism. It challenged the gatekeeping role of traditional media outlets and gave everyday individuals a platform to shape the public conversation.

Yet it was with BuzzFeed, launched in 2006, that Jonah truly cemented his place in history. Beginning as an experimental side project in viral content tracking,

BuzzFeed evolved under his leadership into a media juggernaut that combined entertainment, hard news, and lifestyle content into a model perfectly tuned to the rhythms of social sharing.

BuzzFeed's success rested not on luck, but on Jonah's sophisticated understanding of what made people care, laugh, think, and share. His willingness to blend data science with editorial intuition led to new ways of crafting content, testing ideas, and responding dynamically to audience behavior. In a landscape dominated by static editorial hierarchies, Jonah built an organization that was fast, adaptive, and relentlessly experimental.

His vision did not stop at entertainment. By investing heavily in BuzzFeed News starting around 2012, Jonah demonstrated that viral media companies could also be platforms for serious, impactful journalism. BuzzFeed News' investigations into corruption, global scandals, and political misconduct — particularly during the volatile years surrounding the 2016 U.S. election—

proved that high-quality journalism could coexist with the attention economy, though not without tension and sacrifice.

Jonah's legacy is also shaped by his willingness to confront the challenges posed by a rapidly evolving internet. As advertising models shifted, algorithmic platforms like Facebook and Google tightened their control over audience reach, and public trust in media fractured, he did not retreat into nostalgia. Instead, he pressed forward, seeking new ways to build sustainable business models, integrate emerging technologies like AI, and keep journalism and creativity alive in a climate that increasingly favored polarization and sensationalism.

The integration of artificial intelligence into BuzzFeed's creative operations beginning in 2023 reflected Jonah's enduring belief in experimentation. Rather than treating AI as a threat to human creativity, he approached it as a tool for augmentation — a new brush for the vast canvas of digital storytelling. Through AI-powered quizzes, content generation tools, and editorial enhancements, BuzzFeed continued to embody Jonah's ethos: adapt, create, and connect.

Yet beyond the technologies and business strategies, his most enduring contribution may be cultural. He helped redefine what it means to tell stories online. He showed that humor, emotion, authenticity, and even outrage could serve not just to entertain, but to forge real connections across geography, language, and ideology. He challenged institutions to be more open, media to be more participatory, and audiences to be more empowered.

Through it all, Jonah remained consistent in his core principles: curiosity over conformity, participation over passivity, resilience over reputation.

In the early 2000s, few could have predicted how integral the internet would become to the daily lives of billions. Fewer still would have foreseen that much of the way the modern world communicates — from viral memes and hashtag activism to digital-first journalism

— would bear the fingerprints of a soft-spoken experimenter who, from an MIT lab and later a SoHo office, shaped the tides of culture itself.

Jonah Peretti's story is not simply one of media entrepreneurship. It is the story of how ideas travel, mutate, and inspire in an interconnected age. It is the story of a pioneer who, instead of seizing the spotlight for himself, built platforms that allowed millions of others to find their voices, share their stories, and change the world in ways large and small.

As the internet continues to evolve, his influence will remain embedded in its very fabric — not in monuments or headlines, but in every share, every meme, every story that crosses a border in an instant and binds people together across the vast digital expanse.